SHE DOESN'T LOVE ME. I AM SAD

Poems by:
Derek Porterfield

Published by TNDMTR Publishing a division of TNDMTR

Visit our website at TNDMTR.COM

First published in 2021

This is a book of poetry, but uh, any similarity to real persons, living or dead, is coincidental and not intended. So stop acting like everything is about you, Frank. It isn't. Work on yourself, man.

ISBN 978-1-7370305-0-8

Printed in the United States of America

This book is dedicated to Target Superstores and all of their subsidiaries. You changed my life last year in a cool way.

Thanks.

CONTENTS

SHE DOESN'T LOVE ME. I AM SAD

GUITAR

So I was 16 years old and working in a dollar movie theater in Westgate Mall. It had a strange smell permeating the walls and the seat cushions that sat somewhere between months old pickle juice and a porn shop in the 80s.

It was called "Premiere Cinema", which is hilarious to me.

Premiere was my first job and remains among the most fond memories I have of growing up. The friends I made there were fascinatingly diverse and so unique that each one could serve as a separate chapter in this collection. However, one friend was of greater importance and lasting impact than the rest.

Trey was an usher, the dude that takes tickets and rips them before telling you to file into "theater 2" or whatever.

I worked in concessions and thought that he was by far the strangest human I'd yet met. He had two friends that would occasionally visit and they had strange inside jokes that they would yell at each other.

One had something to do with asking if Trey had any bread.

It was a very gothic, outsider, emo vibe that they had going on, and my still mildly religious and incredibly sheltered view of them was one of confusion and fascination.

After a bit, Trey was promoted to projection. The job came with a pay raise ($7 an hour instead of $5.25) and was by far the coolest part of the theater. I moved to the usher stand (not a pay raise) and spent my days damaging out chocolate almonds by throwing them on the floor and claiming they came out of the box that way so I could eat them, and flirting with the girls that worked there, exuding all of the grace of a giraffe giving birth.

We were a tight knit group and, though he was quiet, the times that Trey would interject into our conversations were hilarious. We became tentative friends, the kind that talk at work about small things and make the lengthy days go by a bit quicker.

I dug him.

It was a slow evening during the week when he came up behind me at the usher stand and without any sort of conversational segway asked, "You wanna be in a band?".

"Hell yea!" I said. I didn't yet curse as much as I do now so "hell" was quite the exclamation. I asked what he played.

"Nothing, really, I could do drums though?" he seemed unbothered by needing an instrument.

"I play guitar." I lied.

I was a guitar *owner*, as my friend Brandon likes to put it. There are guitar players and guitar owners and I fit squarely into that second category.

I had an acoustic from Hastings. It's string action was so far above the fretboard that we took the whole thing apart and shoved folded cardboard into the gap between the body and board to raise it enough to be playable. That is not hyperbole or a joke.

If that thing could have ever sounded good, it would never have happened in my startling inept hands. I knew Wonderwall and exactly three Blink 182 songs. I had learned these to impress girls.

It didn't work.

Trey came to my house the next week and we set up a mishmash of laundry detergent tubs and tupperware for toms and a kick drum. I had a metal cash box that held some of my more treasured belongings that we used as a high hat.

I picked up the Hastings acoustic and we just jammed.

Anyone that has ever played music with other people knows that there doesn't have to be a great amount of talent to afford a certain transcendence while playing. There's an energy of two or more people trying to create together that can fill up a room and is far better than any type of drug high or pleasure on this planet. Seriously, I believe it's why so many musicians turn to substance abuse eventually. That feeling is incredible and I have been chasing it ever since.

That's why I play music. Why I write songs. It's a selfish pursuit of that feeling.

It's also a catharsis of sorts. A therapy for a wounded pride following each subsequent relational failure in my life.

I recognize how most of my music can be distilled to: She doesn't love me. I am sad.
It's a familiar and comfortable tone, like a sweatshirt with holes and faded print that's too cozy to get rid of.
In this book, you'll see a more raw and honest version of me in different phases of my life and my band. Many of these poems were written with full intentions to turn them into music. But, in the words of Patrick Rothfuss, "Music is a temperamental mistress", and I found myself unable to form the right notes to shape the words into songs. Some of these were written during very dark times in my life. Those should be kind of apparent. I promise, I'm doing better now.
I included some lyrics from songs that are currently in progress. They may change a ton by the time you listen to the next record. I've made an effort over the last two years to try and show what my writing process is like and have enjoyed sharing the more inceptive parts of music with all of you. I hope you dig it.
I've put the songs from four of my five records, in chronological order, at the back of this book. The first album, while formative and a huge part of my youth, feels so distant as to be foreign to me now. The songs on that record aren't something I'm ashamed of, but felt out of place in this book. I'll put them on the website in case you'd like to see what seventeen year old Derek wrote about. (hint: it's still girls)
I also found that I missed having lyric booklets and album art to leaf through when I bought a new record. Maybe this will fill the hole.

All of this is a very long winded path towards saying "thank you". If you're one of the original fans from over 15 years ago or if you just found this and thought the cover was cool, I'm glad you're reading or listening. Thanks.
I probably love you.

THE POEMS

Genuine

I'm watching your hair dance and sway against the wind and snow
Your eyes catch the blue of your sweater and I'm home
If these roads still turn towards your room and my car follows them in
I could pray for another page in a spiral pad
I could whisper while trying to scream
You never meant a word you said but I'm damned if that smile was fake
Cause through the harshest wind and behind your fur lined jacket
Your teeth burned a white hot flame into my eyes that chases me to sleep
Even now
Shaking hands pass a note written through tears and hopeful resolve
Folded hurriedly with the chads still hanging
You'll read it in less than half the time it took to write
And that night
You'll pick up your phone
Dial 5 numbers
Hang up
And go to sleep
The next morning you'll never think of that day again but
Every song I chase through the streets of towns I don't know
Each word that eludes my pen and paper
All the notes I've missed while playing your memories for crowds in old bars
When finally put together in a room of cigarettes and eager ears
Form a perfect picture of a day when a snow covered note held promises you couldn't possibly hope to keep
Cause while you rest beneath your covers in a bed I used to know
I stay awake each night hoping for two more digits in your phone
So sleep darling
It's always snowing here
Sleep
My notebooks bleed with who you were
Sleep
While your smile keeps me hoping
Those lips form harsh words for a man that's been willing to listen
But parted ever slightly, when you looked and matched my eyes
I refuse to see that as anything less than
Genuine

Lines

I've written all these lines
You just snort them in the bathroom
My songs are a bad time
Cause every one is about you
You hate to hear me sing
Empty choruses and tired cliches
Mind drained
I never think
Of anything at all but you

Old Friends

That cigarette in your left hand
Fingers marked from the ash and flame
You're looking out the windows of my sedan
Still lost in that daydream

Products of labor

Work until these knuckles bleed
So that
When they drop me down
Six feet deep
By God no one will have a shinier coffin than me

An Autumn Kill

Oh they say it ain't the fall that kills
Just the impact
So I'm keeping an unhealthy distance
Fantasize that look in your eyes could be mine
Avoiding contact as preservation
No offense dear
This happens all the time
It's not that you, yourself aren't special
It's just that every mountain I see is one I need to climb
You don't need that kind of empty in your life
You don't want that sad, hard, truth
That though you may be crying in the morning, darling,
I will
Already be over you

Muse

I can't remember the chords or notes in the songs that I wrote
But I know they were all about you
I threw them away
Each torn crumpled page
Nothing short of perfect would do
For you

Genealogy

They say blood is thicker than the water we're drinking
And the liquor that's killing you and me
But I know better than to embrace tradition,
I'll always choose my friends over family.
And I'm cast so far away from that tree
Thankful that the branches cannot reach
Me

Safe Harbor

I got scared and tied us to shore
But we both know that's not what boats are for
Cut the rope and let us float out to sea

Pop Goes Acoustic

You were another a pop punk love song
I play acoustic and could never sing along
You were a high note in a track I couldn't sing
Above me
A place I tried to find
But never really reached
I could sing to you
Empty platitudes
Something folksy and out of key
I could strum this old guitar
Pretend love isn't so far
Out of reach

Asphalt

Have you ever really looked at the asphalt?
The frozen ocean of cracked tar and spent cigarettes
Empty sonic cups floating atop the tumultuous currents
Tossed carelessly about in the night air
Slow down
I need to soak this moment in
The moonlight on the pavement
Fluorescent paint reflected in dull yellow on an empty street
We sit cross legged on a curb breathing lungs full of warm summer sky
Progressively we all become philosophers
As 1 AM turns to 4 and tired is replaced with awkward energy
Renewed in our vigor we drench ourselves in nostalgia
I want to be a teenager again
I want to drive fast and reckless
I want to dream and still believe that I can be anything
I want to hold hands and tremble on the inside
Kiss her and nervously wonder if I'm doing it right
Curse to feel cool
Sneak out at 2 am
Stomach cheap warm beer and pretend to like it
Play Halo from night until morning without blinking once
Forgetting homework and feeling like it mattered
Curfew at 11 and leaving her house at 10:58
A cafeteria lunch of M&M's and Dr. Pepper
No bills
Crap jobs
Late nights
True friends
A conscience
An unfettered spirit
Our curbside revelations rest above the asphalt on sixth
Though the night is young
Our bodies are not
Sleep defeats a desire to stay and wearily we drive home
Floating on the solid waves of pavement that whisper memories of who I used to be

Derek Porterfield

I'm Just as Think as you Drunk I am

Am I drunk enough for you to speak your mind?
Open up and tell me something beautiful
Whisper your Smirnoff flavored lungs of air into my ever ready ear
Tell me secrets with shaky legs and blurry sight
Slurred words of unending affection
I need that fairy tale love
The kind of "hold-your-hair" and puke love
Full of loud music and cheap 40s
Sharing a cigarette and hating the taste but finishing the damn thing anyway
You trying hard to walk in heels designed for someone with inhumanly small and apparently pointed feet
Me, wishing I'd watched sports center more often as the guys drunkenly argue over some postseason....thingy
That kid, the short one wearing a cape made of napkins he taped together while getting high in the basement
We used to be cool
Romantic to the core
Who needs roses when solo cups are more appreciated?
What are chocolates when you know you'll be puking them up later?
What is love when both people realize
Upon an all too sudden waking, that
Every sweet kiss shared over drunken conversation
Every soft brush of her hand against his
Each promise whispered in back bedrooms of houses
Wasn't real
"Forever" tossed around like cheerios at a daycare
"Love" spoken as a true thespian
"Me" overused like blood in a Taratino film
"Oh god" spoken just before that glaring buzzkill of stomach acid and cheap McDonalds take out
They say in wine there is truth
The only truth I saw was the consistency of my mistakes
The gospel for those drunken lovers tangled beneath blankets that reek of axe body spray and spilt beer, is this:
That lover won't remember your name the next day
That lover won't call until she realizes her purse is in your car
She wants you drunk, quiet and gone
So
I'm inebriated enough to listen but not speak
Drunk enough that I won't remember what you really think of me

Air Bags

I don't want to break your fall
I don't want to be the one to say I'm sorry
I just need to feel your heart
Tell me once and maybe I'm going crazy
But I feel the lie and inside I know I'm wrong
I can't ever say I'm sorry

Caught

She said she's looking for something that she can't find in me
A sense of closure on the love we shared
Would taste so sweet
And I'm lying to my journals and every single friend
Telling both I've never loved and that I never will again
Cause her tongue is dry as it slips, gentle, in my mouth
And her hand grabs hair on the back of my neck
Bodies move without a sound
We stay familiar at a distance that's reserved for enemies
Talking as lovers
Remaining only friends that share each other's sheets
Your hand in mine still feeling his
I'm beginning to remember why I tried to forget
A love like ours needs time to heal
So much time to heal
So much damn time to heal
And I am
Who you dreamed about
But God, I think I'm lost
I am
The one you wished for but
But never really caught

Bad Words

I used to whisper
Hushed appellations strained across anxious chords
I never cursed
Just focused all four letters in glances of daggers and swords
But now that I'm older those quiet secrets and unspoken feelings are escaping lips that still ache from the bonds I've kept across their flesh for so long
Listen closely my friends
These are the things I've felt but never said in song

Sextant

Always navigating the uncertain
Try to hide inside
Away from what's hurting
Away from the worst of it
Oh but I'm sure
Darling
I promise
We could be great
If the world fades away
If everything changed
Oh someday
We could be great
If everything fades
Everything fades
Away

Lost Boy

I'm feeling my age now
A little more each day
When I wake I'm still
So tired
So broken down
Feeling my age now and I'm over
Getting older all the time
And I'm so
I'm so down

Old Man Wallace

I've never been all that good at guitar
But I wanted to play
You said I wouldn't make it very far
But neither will this sad excuse for transportation I call a car
So let's load her up
And drive until we can't anymore
We were just a couple kids with dreams bigger than their talent
Chasing away those sad realities of maturity
With songs we can barely play
Wish I'd known then
What I know now
That these are the days you drink about
When you end up however old that I am now
The days get shorter it doesn't get better
So glad you broke free from this town's cheap tether
I can't recall your face
I just remember your name
And all the things we said we'd be

LOVE

When I was in eighth grade I fell in love for the first time.
Her name was Ashley and I did her homework so that she would talk to me. It was a symbiotic relationship of the sort I would grow to pursue almost exclusively as I grew up. Much to my own detriment.
Ashley wrote the longest note on the back of my yearbook, and at thirteen, that was as good an admission of our fated romantic affections as anything. We talked for hours on the phone over the summer and I remember, distinctly, those somersault turnings in my stomach when she smiled at me.
But, remarkably, I was wrong.
That wasn't love anymore than it was love when I first tasted a REAL cappuccino.
It was close.
It was my first flirtation with what love was, but I had yet to really grab hold of that deeper affection that Ed Sheeran was always singing about.
Then there was Amy. My first actual girlfriend. We went on dates and talked about futures and toyed with the idea of marriage. The first time I ever held hands was with Amy. We were at the mall. It was raining, her nails were freshly painted in a checkered black and white pattern and we ran through the downpour to my 1983 Silverado. Soaked and laughing, we held hands the entire way back to her house. Basically like The Notebook.
That was love.

Or, I thought it was. Until I met Sarah. We worked at Marble Slab, both of us on the closing shift. The first time I said the "fuck" word was when I yelled at her ex-boyfriend on the phone and told him to "fuck off" as he'd been bugging her and making her miserable for the past week.
She thought that was cool and we started to spend a lot of time enjoying each other's company. I followed Sarah to college and believed in my heart that we would be together until George Bush started World War 3. Obviously, I was mistaken on a couple of fronts.
I chased other girls with varying degrees of success and danced precariously close to that feeling of love. But never touched it.
I've been engaged.
Twice.
That was expensive.
And certainly *felt* like love.
I won't expound upon those relationships out of respect for two people that anyone reading this could potentially know. But they both are wonderful humans, to whom I owe a great deal of growth.
But again, that love, while full of parallel emotions to the actual thing, was only a facsimile of what I felt when I first held my daughter.
Hazel was born when I was 25 years old and making $8 an hour as an IT guy. My first thought upon holding her was how absolutely perfect she was. Fragile, impossibly small and terrifyingly dependent on me. I was flooded with responsibility and this whole-bodied desire to give her the best possible life that I could.
My second thought was about how damnably poor I was.
Hazel is a love unlike any I've ever felt. Her mind and her heart are so full of wonder and light and I find myself bereft of proper adjectives when attempting to express how deeply grateful I am for her in my life.
I wake up every day attempting to work and live and love in such a way that I can make her proud and help her to grow and become the best version of herself as she begins to discover what it is that defines and shapes her own reality.
My job, as a dad, is one of unconditional love. Of support forever and always. A love so profound that it shattered my entire paradigm and reshaped me into someone else entirely. Someone better.
That was love.
The kind Ed sings about.
Love of the sort that drives men to accomplish great things.
I have felt that for Hazel.
I have felt that only one other time.
Ironically, it was within this past year, while writing this book. The circumstance is inconsequential. It amounted to very little, as love is not a one sided affair. Unrequited though it was, it's existence was profound and alarming and humbling.

Realizing that I could feel something so strong, unconditioned and complete for another person besides my own daughter was a revelatory experience and I'm thankful.
Thankful to have passed a great deal of time in the company of someone with whom I was discovering such an intrinsically beautiful part of my own soul. A part I had long since believed was gone.
I don't care if that sounds dramatic. This is a poetry book.
I've not lived a terribly difficult life by most measures. I am privileged in ways that go beyond just my skin color and gender and I recognize how self absorbed, and even tone-deaf, the despair of my music and poems can sound in the context of that privilege.
But that's why we write about love. It's a rare, universal experience that people from any walk can hear and recognize. Something you can read and mutter to yourself, "felt".
Or, "same."
"This".
Whatever.
It's a communal bond and I hope that something in here tugs at the frayed ends of your heart strings. And if you, like I used to, believe that the more profound parts of romance are in your past with people you met when your hormones played a larger role in your decision making, I think you're wrong.
I was.
With startling regularity throughout most of my life.
To steal a line from John Mayer, "You just gotta wait your turn. She's out there, he's out there. They're just learning what to contrast you against."
I hope your turn comes up soon. Cause you're a badass. And I probably love you.

(But like a normal amount)

Baby Don't Hurt Me

She was light at the end of a dark tunnel
She was a train
I'm collapsed on the tracks and run over and bloodied
Vulnerable all over again.

There's a reason that all of the metaphors for love are so violent.
It's not tulip fields and rays of warm sunshine
Or the way that air smells on the first night
Of fall
It isn't that first sip of warm coffee or the electric shock of fingertips
interlaced in a car racing too fast to beat curfew
Love isn't the startled inhale of winter wind as she wraps you in her arms
under snowfall and Christmas Time lighting

No.

It's not your sympathetic nervous system set alight when her eyes meet
yours or
The gentle flip that your stomach makes each time you hear her voice.

No.

It's a man
Laying in pools of his own blood
Losing light from his eyes
Love, friend
Love is the knife in his stomach
Love is taking him away
Love is all that drains

Southern Gospel

She said there isn't a God this side of the Mason-Dixon
I had to disagree
I've never been much for religion
But when I catch her eyes, that's God staring back at me.

Siren Songs and Sharp Stones

We were both caught up in the discordant resonance of our own folly.
Your eyes the siren song leading me from whatever safe haven I thought worth chasing,
To be caught on rocks my heart would never begrudge spending it's last beats bleeding upon.
I know, deep in the marrow of my being, that you have become part of me. A piece of metallic shaving ever present and biting in my mind, working to burrow its way deep inside.
But damned be the distance between this vessel and your siren song. The hollows of my life echoing the saccharine tones of lust and love and passion from the sweet vibrato of your chords. You are magic, and I never believed in witchcraft. You are God Herself and I claimed to be agnostic but now...
The sun sets and my path remains alight in the brightness and perfection of you.

Love

I want to see every film you've ever loved
Hear the songs that caused new creases in your brain
I want to hold your hand in every quiet moment and listen to your pain
Because
You are every beautiful line in all of the best poems
You hold my world entire in the palm of your hand
I know now that God exists and that He cares for me so deeply
Cause somehow I found you again

Linger (do ya have to?)

I don't hit it and quit it
I hit it and linger
I'm actually a pretty bad singer
And girl I'd write you a song
The emotion from your love potion is so fucking strong
And I long for just the touch of your lips and
The pressure of your hips
Those fingertips in my hair
Move close to me
You're all I see
The world could ignite and I won't care
You're there when I dream
You incredible thing
Love sick I'll stick with ya and give ya a ring
Simple seams
In the clothing you wear
Another piece of you that I wanted to tear
Up
Soft as your skin
Strong as your mind
I'm caught up and punch drunk thinking about those thighs and your eyes
drenched in experience
Lives full but meaningless
Without the bracing mistakes we make while faking love and chasing sex
I'm hearing this
Full blast on the speakers we listen to
Screaming those stupid tunes
Love bringer
Please
Darling please
Just let me linger

Tape

Tape me back together and
Tell me it gets better and
Teach me how to live through the cracks in the seams
Hold me when the pieces slip and
Hate the ones that love and dip and
Hang on when life loses luster in sun beams

But honest when you fill me up
The tape doesn't stick enough
I'm spilling my guts and you're watching me bleed
Forgive me
You were a hope I hadn't felt in years
Too much to carry alongside your own dreams and fears
My anxious affection is a hard learned lesson
Calluses built over eight short months
Not years

God Bless Target

I just want to send a girl into hysterics
She could tell me that I'm clever and she likes my lyrics
Read me all her poetry late at night
Visit art shows like a couple of hipsters
Kiss her with tongue, yea she's making her hips work
In flared out corduroy pants
Someday she'll dance with me
They say that love is for the young and the dumb
Well you're young and I'm dumb
We could work it out
It's a damn hard thing to navigate
I still think that we should date
We could work it out
I want a girl that doesn't mind that I don't talk to my parents
In a couple of years she can ask where my hair went
Growing old we could hold each other tight
I was always told when you know you know
I didn't believe em then but now I know
You're the girl that I've been chasing my whole life
And I found you on the endcap of the aisle
You were looking at your cell phone and your smile
Drew me in
You drew me in
So
God bless Target
God damn your ex
Tell me that you love me over a text
I don't care what happens next
If you're here with me
Just be here with me

Are we dating?

She called me late it was Thursday
The bars were all starting to close
I said "don't you think you need sleep dear"
She said "yes, but I don't want to go home"
So we each became home
Two vessels without a harbor
Each the other's mother or father
A safe place to feel less alone

Every Summer Breath

We were jamming Taylor Swift in some parking lot east side of town
You were struggling with the words
Slurred speech we were coming down
And that sound
Of your laugh mid song
And the air
Filling our lungs with summer
Tangled tongues craving one another
I won't breathe a word of what we said
Keep that night safe in heart and head
Lay awake still wishing you in this bed
I'll never speak of what you said
Words so different than what you meant
So young, in what we thought was love
So bold, infatuated, intoxicated
You will always be
Every Summer breath

CESILY

I'll admit I'm kinda over the line
I've asked you too many times before
You're probably sick of all the stray dogs always scratching
Scratching at your door

But I swear to you I'm better now
Head clearer I can see
Oh God I see
I know I asked you far too much before and that
Well, that's on me
But please

Tell me someday you could change your mind
And see it differently
Tell me someday you and I
Could make an effort
Try to find
That longing that's reflected equally

Not just from me

Modern Romance

She only likes me when she's drinking
She'll only touch me when she's high
She tells me softly that she loves me
But it's only ever in reply

Steer (not the animal)

You got this steering wheel just left of center in your chest
I've been driving us off course but giving it my best
I guess
The world isn't quite as it seems
I guess it was you that should have been guiding me

House So Empty Need a Centerpiece

Never bought any of that astrology bullshit
You tell me I'm a Libra
The description doesn't fit
But now
I'm looking at the stars more often
I can see them in your eyes
I'm looking for the signs more often
And I
Can tell that you and me were meant to be
And I
Didn't believe in fate
Until you showed it to me
I didn't know a love like this could exist
Until a Leo rejected my kiss
I could get used to this
I always thought those charts were kinda foolish
You asked when I was born and said
You couldn't believe I'd dated a Taurus
Now I'm
Seeing those signs more often
Misreading your eyes
Looking to the sky more often
Cause I
Can tell
It was always you and me
And I
Chased you with all my heart
So foolishly
I believed all at once that love exists
I swear to God
I swear to God that it did
I should be used to this

This isn't a sonnet

Shall I compare thee to a summer's day?
When all about us is naught but rain?
When storm and famine and plague do knock
I wish so truly your bed I could rock
With passionate bodies so intertwined
Sharing the buzz of mediocre wine
Entangled tongues like some young teens
Passing time during the world's last quarantine
Alas, I'm left to flirt from afar
And scream infidelities from the safety of my car

Paint her

I'm a blind, sad, painter
Just feeling this shit out
You were a canvas, colors tacit
All synesthetic sounds
Beauty felt before it's ever seen
Don't let these clumsy hands near your perfect frame

Irony

I once chased a girl, she said my clothes were dated
Complained that I always stayed sedated
After 5 with alcohol and poetry
She wasn't wrong I just thought that I was woke
Desperate for attention in a band that's just one bloke
That's me
It's me
I'm tired and apathetic
Cliche and educated
Wasting privilege and talent equally
Then whining on my records about how everybody hates me
Is that Irony?
I don't know what that means
She said, as she grabbed her coat
I struggle with affection I told her but I misspoke
It's just that I can't love the ones that love me
Despite years of therapy
This new girl seems like just the thing
I might even buy a third engagement ring
Then get down on my knee in someplace pretty
I can write another record when she finally leaves me
Is that irony?
You're the wrinkles in the corners of my eyes
My arrhythmic chest
Electricity on my arms
And I can't stop chasing you
I wrote you a song a long time before
You never heard it cause you don't fuck with me anymore
Honest I don't blame you
But I can't stop chasing you
I won't stop chasing you
It feels like love to me
Sounds like love to me
Is that irony?

Oxygen

And there's no fire
Burning down inside her
Her soul is empty
Just like me
Oh but I find a comfort
In the resonant thunder
In the chaos beneath
Her apathy
In the nothing
No glow
No flame
No spark
In the darkness
That would pull us both apart
In the hollow
Attached by echos and marrow
That sends chills pressed against my own
She calls to something deep in my bones
We may be empty but we
Aren't alone
We aren't alone
We embrace the empty but we won't be
Alone

Ms. Me

She says do you miss me I say
Only when I wake up in the morning
Or go to bed at night
And those places in between the two
You are on my mind
Only when I'm driving
Down the streets we once knew
Or when I'm cuddled up with someone else
That smells like you used to
I don't miss you
My lips are never far from your name
You live, so full of resplendent wonder
Forever in my brain.

Co-Dependence

She said we should drive until the lights stop hurting
Harder lessons we avoided learning
The world spins differently the older you get
I guess
Lost balance I'm still trying to get a grip

She said she lost something inside of herself
We all have our own hell
The world breaks harder as a father
I guess
Lost touch with reality, fell out of step

I need a taste of you
Something to hold onto
I need a breath of smoke free air
These lungs God gave me hate it here

Unfinished Love Songs

I want to kiss the air that floats above you
Taste your lips and lick the gloss right of you
Whisper all the places we could go
But you said no

Orange Peel

I found a piece of orange peel yesterday
One of the ones you threw at me
Mid conversation
Devolving from talking into full on battle stations
Laughing and hurling food across my kitchen
It was what?
Two?
Three in the morning?
I woke up yesterday thinking about that night
Then made coffee and saw it.
Under the cabinet, tucked away
Dried out and dead
A reminder
You were real
I think
This has been really fucking tough

I don't think

I don't think
Anyone loves me anymore
No I don't think
You ever think
About me anymore
Cause we were love
But all that's gone
At first light every morning
Darling you were dawn
And now you're gone
So far gone
You don't think
When you talk to me anymore
No you don't think
Before you speak
I'll walk right out the door
Swear to god that I'm worth more
But we were love
How is that gone?
Tears spent useless
Your shit's out on the lawn
And I am done
Oh I could love you
Long enough
For you to grow so tired
Of me
I could keep loving you more
Maybe more once you leave
But we were love
In all it's awkward forms
We were love
An open heart still torn
We were love
Darling
Love
And now you're gone

Catchlights

I think it's the light
And the way it catches in your eyes and ignites every color inside of them
all at once
But that gives the light too much credit
The praise belongs with you
Cause for every ray of sunshine
You match it back with two

She's Liam Neeson

She's crossed her arms
A diamond on
Whatever finger means a man has caught her
Are you home safe?
Someone's arms around your waist?
Someone's lips soft on your face?
Are you safe?
I won't pray for grace
God placed
His only child on a bloody altar
With crossed beams and pierced limbs he never blinked, never faltered
No there isn't any forgiveness for the awful
That I've done
I'll lay awake and choke on all the silence
Her eyes keep my sight ever blurred with self hatred and violence
You deserve the love of a better man
Pursued you just to spite that ring on your hand
To prove to one or both of us that I'm better than
The one that shares your bed at night
The better man
He's the better man
I'm a hollow sinner chasing angels in the alley
Your porcelain perfection my hands will just sully
My lips are laced with silver and my blood runs cold
You told me that I'm wasting air
I hope I never grow old
You say I'm wasting air
I was far too bold
You say I'm wasting air and you aren't wrong
I'm a coward and a liar singing hollow love songs
I'm a coward and a liar singing shallow love songs
I'm a coward
I'm a liar
These are only love songs

Say you love me

You could lie and say you love me
And then just leave me like my mother
You could tell me that your feelings for me
Are unlike any other
I'm so used to the fallout
I feel lost now
I'm losing sleep
The truth is
I don't need any of you
As much as you need me
I don't need anybody else
Half as much as they need me

Hate

They should write songs about the way
The screen of your phone illuminates your face
Those perfect eyes dilated wide
Staring into the stream in a daze of absent daydream
With you
The edge of this bed never felt closer
Tired eyes and mind just wishing someone in your place
With you
The drive home is never longer
Park this car and brace for the impact
Smoke out of this doorway
The fire in your eyes with passion you only find in hate
Yes, I've known love
But this is my first brush with
Hate

GOD

I grew up in a very religious home. We were church of christ, which meant that worship was bereft of the live show instrumentation that's so popular today. You get rock concerts and I had elderly women singing acapella gospel tunes in a vibrato that would crack crystal if life were more like the cartoon that I wish it was.

I drew a lot, and made a bunch of militarized airplanes with elaborate guns during service in my sketchbook.

So, it wasn't all bad.

Ours was an evangelical faith. Many lessons were focused on spreading the "good news". That news being, that if you were more like me (and by extension, Jesus), you wouldn't have to burn in hell for eternity. I believe, deep in my bones, that evangelism is what killed the modern church. The very concept of approaching anyone that doesn't feel or believe the things you do with the idea of "converting" them is foolish on its face. Assuming that your views and understanding of God and faith and the Bible are the correct ones and that *bilions* of people that came to a different conclusion aren't only wrong, but will be condemned to an eternity of tortuous suffering, isn't the best way to increase church membership. Or perhaps more pointedly, to increase tithing.

My dad was a deacon. I played with the preacher's kids before and after services and grew up praying before meals and before bed.

So I was "in it". For a long time.

But as I grew older, I started to really look into the lessons I was being taught. The book that I'd memorized decent chunks of was being used, in large part, to justify prejudice and hate.

Homosexuals make you uncomfortable? Boy do I have a verse for you! (Leviticus 18:22)

Is the president one that you like? Here's a verse telling you to respect him. (Hebrews 13:17)

Don't like the president? Jesus' entire arc is one of rising up against corrupt leadership.

In the wrong hands, religion can be a weaponized tool of assimilation. Removing even the hint of critical thinking.

Aligning your ideals with manipulated scriptures allows a subset of the population to work with you, without question. God, of course, must be the one that appointed you.

And it's in this push to spread the faith, and to condemn those that fall outside of it, that the church has lost its way.

Setting aside the egregious sums of money funneled through these tax shelters claiming to house god, we should, at the very least, be questioning any message that doesn't revolve around loving with such earnest conviction that your belief system is apparent in action.

I remember hearing, repeatedly, in WASP circles I grew up in, how homeless people were just using the money for drugs.

Ok.

I don't care what someone does with my money once I have given it to them. If I didn't have a roof, I imagine drugs would be a pretty great way to feel a brush with happiness before crashing back into the horrors of my own reality. My life isn't theirs and to behave in a way that withholds aid because of a preconceived notion about how they might try and numb their own pain is completely antithetical to Christian living.

I don't talk about my own faith at all. I sing about alot of this junk in songs and poetry but the way that I've always viewed it is this: God is the exact same thing as sex. I think it's great that you have it, but I don't need to hear all the details unless we are SUPER close. It's a personal thing, and insofar as that's true, it should stay private.

The way I know that you have great sex with your wife, is in the way that she smiles when you look at her, and how you hold hands through the super market or whisper those dirty jokes in each other's ears in public spaces. The way I know that you love God is in how you treat the wait staff at Olive Garden, how easily you love people you've never met and how generous you are to anyone that may be in need.

I know, I'm basically preaching here, but this is important to me. And it's important that anyone of faith reading this book might be able to self-reflect a bit and read the words of a kid who was once at the choir boy levels of faithfulness, then became evangelically atheist, and now, has discovered his own spirituality far, far away from the multimillion dollar church buildings and bible thumping Christians that I grew up with. I don't believe in hell, but if you think that's where I'm headed, maybe that says more about you than me.

Times I Pray

I only pray when I feel afraid
So I talk to God all night and all day
But I can't ever hear what you say
Goddamn what did you say?
I only pray when I feel scared
The consistency leaves my hands bare
My voice raw, from screaming into the wall
Cause God never talks
No She won't talk to me

Lies

She told me God was just a song you sang in church pews
A hollow vessel where we all go to die
She said that Jesus was just an effort to wear others' shoes
But her religion wasn't angels in the sky
No her religion wasn't built on
Lies

My best curse words are about you

Dear fucking Jesus Christ
I looked into your eyes and saw the northern lights
So barren and so cold
But there's a haunting, perfect beauty in your soul
Mary Mother of God
You are every anxious thought
The tired light fading from my view
There's a lovely, simple, subtle, perfect, intoxicating beauty inside you

Bad Poetry

You were all my bad poetry
Empty lines and worthless imagery
I was a kid with simple thoughts and simpler dreams
You took that away from me
You took the bravest parts of me
You were the metaphors I slurred
An angry bird
In the cage I built us both
Confounding, confining and broken
All the same
I hope to God you realize who you've become
I hope you drown in your ego and lust
I hope the blood from your dagger stains the fashion and false passions
You faked your fucking smiles long enough to get cut
You just haven't drank enough to tell me that we're done yet
Muster up your courage
I was just a lie you kept
A hopeful heart inside your chest

Mirror

Her house was filled to the brim with mirrors and trinkets
designed to fill spaces companionship should have
It wasn't a home so much as a showroom
A museum through which one floats about
With self admiration as the lone companion

Duck

I curse more than I ought to
But much less than I would like
It's this awkward balance beam of society and a wasted life
And just like mine you were trying your best
To keep your head above the water
Think I'll stay under just a little longer

Icarus

We keep holding it together like
Two birds of a feather like
Two kids who don't know better
I'm
Icarus without his wings and
You're still the only sunlight that I've seen
You perfect thing
You're angelic holding both my missing wings
Holding it together like
The glue on both our hands and I'm
Chasing our romance
Tasting nothing but regret and
I'll fly like Icarus without his wings
Just hubris and awkward energy
Love hasn't been that kind to me
You're too beautiful
And I'm this ugly thing
I'm a broken dream
It's just a bit of bad timing
Another example
I'm a bad mistake
And you're the brightest star I struggled so damned long to see
You're too good for me
You're too good to be
You're too good for me
I tried holding it together
Just chasing missing feathers
I could glue us back together and
Fly as though the world was ours to see
But dreams are empty things
Like you and me
The whole sky turned to fire from perfect blue
And I've got nothing left to hold onto
So I'm holding onto you

Counterfeit

Every pretty picture is obscene
I'm living life inside this dream
And all I hoped for was a lie that came true upon waking
Pallid palettes and semitonal sounds
Cracked edges of the heaven I thought I'd found
And all that I wished for was built from cardboard
For the life that I've been faking

Weeds on Your Tomb

The man that mows the grass above your coffin
Spends more time with you than I do
You feel his footsteps much more often
And I'm sorry
For the things I don't do
For you
A boy cries alone in the lobby
Says he'll be fine in just a few
I struggle with the words to try and help him
Another way in which I always relied on you
The girl down the street from your apartment
Fixes her hair like you used to
I catch her eyes now much more often
Disappointed, that she isn't you
I guess maybe I'm just scared
Wholly unprepared
This life I live without you isn't bright enough for me
It shouldn't be a bother but it is
He left weeds near your tomb
And I can't bring myself to do,
Anything about it

Raw Men

Eating Ramen on your front porch watching the sunrise
Waiting for God to come
But he never comes.

Goodfellas

I'm sinking like a body in the hudson bay
Chains wrapped around my ankles and I'm struggling to breathe
Yea my lungs are filling faster
Than my head can comprehend

And I'm sorry
For the things that I can't do
Yea I'm sorry
For telling you I love you
When I never follow through
I'm sorry
I'm sorry
I'm sorry

Ariana was right

I know now that God must be a woman
Always begging for attention
Asking me to listen
But when I need Her
Absent
God has to be a woman
Omniscient but begging for more
Scraps of Her eternity littering my floor
My face contorted and sick to the core
Yes
I have met God
She just doesn't like me anymore

Daughter

You'll forever be the catchlights in my eyes
The parts of me the resonate so bright
The only thing I've ever done that's right
When it's dark out, dear
I pray you find the light
You'll find the light
Push past all the dark and fight
Know that dawn always follows night
So please forgive me
I don't deserve the honor
Of calling you my daughter
But I'll try my best to be
Better than my parents were to me
You're the lullabies I could never seem to write
The songs that calm a heart so used to flight
The most lovely purpose in my entire life
When it's beautiful, you're the reasons why
Love, you're the light

Rites

Every piece of paper
Just a bit more sacred
For the absence of our names
And each vow that never crossed our lips
Remains more true than fingertips
On the sweetest curves above your hips
Playing now only on strings
Just wishing you hear me sing
Through the airwaves playing tunes
Imperfect songs that I've written
For you.

Settling

Dance like no one gives a shit
Cause they don't
The world isn't your stage
Nor these people your muse
You go round and round counting fingers down
Of the friends that you can use
And abuse
You are the laughter in dark hallways
So unsettling
So unsettling
Any one who is with you
Is settling

Hollow

Oh I'm hollow
You're the space that fills my empty
Oh I'm broken
You're the pills I thought could fix me
Promise me one thing
Swear that you're real
Promise me you won't disappear
On me
You never call me when you're sober
Begging baby please come over
But we can't fuck away the empty
These shots just blur our thinking
We were never thinking
Eating flashbulb fires
Burnt out but never tired
Up late but still wired
We were a punch drunk melody
I'll buy what you're selling me
High on fallacy
Chasing me for my salary
I don't care who it is that fills me
I'm tired
So tired of being empty

The Tombstone of James Garner

The whole world is a stage
I hope you've found your place
Between those things that steal her sleep
And demons held at bay in the tumult of your sea
You're shallow water and she's face down
Only faith can make the young drown
You are leaves beneath the feet of soldiers wanting familiar soil
The foreign earth they just can't trust
You are dust
A tool that gathers rust
Unable to serve your purpose crushed
By hands gifted in ways that you wish that you could be
The wind exhaled by factories on hills
Wasted potential, cancer in lungs now filled
With you
You are rotten wood
Unstable
Hushed words never understood
When they lower your body six feet into earth
I hope that you're still alive
Still breathing inside
I pray that it rains that day
A torrid, relentless rain
Let you try and take one last bow
And then
I want to hear you drown

Purpose

I hope that someday you find this purpose
Someday you receive
All of the perfect and simple beauty
That you gave to me
I'm not too familiar with god
And never counted much on grace
But I'll be damned if you aren't an angel
With the kindest most perfect face
Tell me you won't mind starting over
That you might like to have a go
At making ends meet with me
Burying our apathy
So we might someday build a home

Tower of

We made out on the floor of my kitchen
The tile floor is uncomfortable but in a way that you don't notice until afterwards because she's so alarmingly and disarmingly beautiful.
And it's not just the drinks
Though I'm sure there were a few
And it's certainly not the lighting
That fluorescent bulb is always such a terrible hue
But that wasn't what what drew me in
So many people reference smiles.
And sure, at 2am smiles and similes are like cab rides and leather seats
A hand in glove or other cliches
I failed to say how I felt and she was perfect.
She was perfect until she wasn't
Until she wouldn't stop drinking
And initial elation gave way to exhaustion
Until she wouldn't stop talking about her ex
I'm not that man that you end up with I'm just the one that's next
No I'm not the one who shares your bed at night,
I'm just the one you text
I'm not the man you end up with
I'm just the one that's next.

I'm not even guarded, not so much anymore. I'm just a book that you pick up and put back on the shelf as you look for something else in the store

THE ALBUMS

WASTED YOUTH AND OTHERS' DREAMS

This album was recorded in a backhouse. My buddy Brandon lived in an efficiency off of I-27 and agreed to record us out of a kindness that I consider to be pretty rare, and perhaps foolish? I hadn't ever used a click (metronome) before and trying to teach me to stay on time, I imagine, was a special sort of hell. We would regularly take breaks to practice kung fu in the back yard and walk down to the Taco Bell on Washington to grab food. I've recorded a lot and in some really cool studios, but that time, in a backhouse with a gas leak that permeated your clothes and probably obliterated several of my already dwindling brain cells, was probably my favorite.

When I screwed up a take, Brandon was always chill. He'd stop the recording and pause before telling me, "I think you've got a better one.". That served as a mantra of sorts throughout big chunks of my life.

To this day, it's the way I like to approach encouraging someone to do something over.

"You've got a better one".

This was also my last time recording with Trey as a member of the band. This is a very special record to me and represents a time in my life that was so pure in it's naive aspirations. I hope you dig it.

Fourth of September

I promised you the world
And delivered in a way
I hope the bracelet in your dresser
Haunts you every single day
Bubble gum and a puzzle piece
An empty box, your inner peace
The love we sold out to ourselves, well
It cheapens everything
It cheapens you and me
It's the fourth of September
God you won't remember
Anything I ever said
Cause come February
You're getting married
And I won't mean anything to you
When he took you out to the stars
Did he tell you all the things that you wanted to hear?
And when he picked up his guitar
Did he play your favorite songs like I did?
Tell me that he makes you happy
Tell me that he fills the hole that I so willingly stole from your heart that day
It's getting closer and closer to June
I'm taking down pictures of you
I knew this day would someday come
I just didn't expect it so soon
You're fitting your wedding dress
Always tried so hard to impress
And look at you now
Just look at you

Austin

We spent ten hours in the car
With your hand in mine
The Austin skyline fell apart
With you by my side
I know its been years but please tell me that
I remember Austin
I remember late nights
Long cries on your driveway
Midnight kisses and SNL
The Simple Life almost every single night
That Paris Hilton's a riot while we kept quiet on the couch
The sixth street lights chased the sky
And your eyes caught fire
Turned away, from every sleazy bar
And the coffee keeps us wired all night
I know its been years but darling, please tell me that
I always remember Austin
(quietly walked these streets)
Always remember every late night when you would sneak into my bed I remember every word you said
(dancing just you and me)
And All those words you whispered in my ear coming in so loud and clear
(quiet laid on your lawn)
"Forever" seemed much longer then
(mascara and tears on my arm)
You know that I will always, always remember Austin

Crimson

I'm tired of listing
All of my faults
And I'm tired of testing
This branch I'm on to see when I might
Fall
We will write
Stories to the ones we love
We'll sing
Songs about the heartache we endured
And these stars will crash around us
But all is lost to crimson in the end.
I'm tired of lying
To pass myself as safe
I'm tired of evading
This sleep that keeps me trapped here in this
Place

Red Heron

Where have you gone to my friend?
I sift through the ashes left from our once burning bridge
Where is that woman that I trusted?
I turned round twice and fear that I might have lost you now
I miss you
So if you're listening on some distant radio and
Hear my voice cracking in 5.1 audio know
Only that I miss you
Realize that I care
Understand I'll always love you thanks for being there
For being there
Are you happy where you are now my friend?
I pour through letters thought about, never sent
Are your thoughts about me adjusted?
The friend you let too close but never should have trusted
I miss you
Through four bad girls and six long years
You listened to me and you caught my tears
In a cold car blaring indie rock and roll
I was the hand you took but were forced to fold
We were young and naïve but we all were thieves back then
I was young and naïve but we all were thieves back then
I'm so sorry my friend
I need the girl who called me "gorgeous"
(I've always been right here)
I need the girl who taught me music as a better way to live
(look around you I'm still here)
I need the girl whose tears could crush this tired soul
(I've always been right here but dear, oh where did you go?)
I need the cure that only she could hold for me
I miss you.
(I miss you)
Where are you?

The Mask

You're smooth like Sinatra
With a heart like Oliver Stone
You're gray like the skies when the clouds try to hide
Their truth from everyone
You're classic in the way
That everyone knows your face
But the name just slips the mind
And that book you hide your face behind tells truth
We've been trying to find
You're dead like Elvis
But you're cute like Marilyn Monroe
You're read like a book but it looks like your cover is blown
Tell me who you think that I should be
The mask I wear is the one you handed me
Tell me who you think that I've become
I'm only trying to be what you wanted

Cuts and Scars

And the opening line
From that song on your mind
Won't help all of this go away
Cause no music sounds pure
Like the way that you were
So just stare at the ceiling and pray
It'll be okay
It'll be okay
Cut out the painful and leave just the obvious
Surface cuts don't mean anything
And these bonds that you break with your dull razor blades
Serve only to sweep you beneath
Yeah they'll sweep you beneath
And the marks and the scars
Like tire tracks from cars
That are racing from forearm to wrist
The numbness is calming
But nothing can harm you, quite as well
Or as often as this
The poems from authors who claim to know pain
Keep pounding at your aching head
The words flow so freely
But It's you who'll be keeping
All the answers you've hidden oh, so far away
So lay down the daggers that you've brandished so well
And put all your trust in me
You may feel alone but darling this wound
Requires some attending
I'll hold the scarred wrist
I'll hold you and listen
Know everything will be okay
Okay

The Drink

Am I that drink that you won't set down?
Am I the high that won't let you come back to the ground?
Am I that dream that keeps you up these sleepless nights?
You whisper to me "my dear you are
all of these things"
So take your lies and toss them in my tired mind
I'll hand you the mirror
And pray to God that all of this will be clearer
Through broken glass and empty sentiments
You are the reason for the pain you feel and yet you seem content
I am not the brother you once loved
No I am not the friend you framed on your desk
I am an animal caged and angry
Yeah I am just another wasted breath
Oh my god
Forgiveness is a word so foreign
Forgiveness is a drink served stale
Forgiveness is a lie we both believed
Forgiving our own naivety
Forgive the sins that I've done
Forgive the things I can't take back
I am the drink that you can't put down
I am the very air that chills your aching bones
You are the malice in the heart of the weak
You are the attack from the God you seek
You are the air beneath the ocean floor
You are the pain that I can't feel anymore

Four AM

Its four AM and there's a storm rollin in of the coast line
And you know how those storm clouds explode late at night
I saw you leaving through the window
Let me know when you get home
Let me know that you're alright
If you need a place to stay
You know my door is always open
Got the blanket by the fire and a box of wine
Let's make this, let's make this
A beautiful night
A vessel silhouettes across the distant sea
I see the sun's about to rise
I can feel my nerves creepin up
Swear I haven't exhaled since late last night
Let me know that you're alright
Let's make this unforgettable
We will be rain and fall
Sun kissed tears from the eyes of God
We will be rain and...

London

Lets run away
Hands clasped tightly and
Let's take a train
Travel to London
And at night
We could count the stars
One for every moment that my restless heart is dreaming of yours
London can't shine
Dull hues of browns and grays
And on this moonless night
That hides the man I thought was watching over me
So goodbye
Good luck
So long
I'm still struck
With the girl who took my breath away
So will you be the lungs I gave away?
So willingly
Let's build a bridge
Put down the axe babe
I'll take the hint
But I won't stop trying
And in time
We might could fix this
But the tools I have lay broken beside you and
Will you be the air that I can't seem to grasp?
And will you take me home?

Prophet

I asked a prophet to show me the way
He said "You wouldn't understand"
I begged forgiveness
Turned every page
In a book that didn't make sense
So I ran down the streets, with tears in my eyes, calling out your name
I'm praying to the stars and cars, that you will understand me
But I'm running away again, calling out to you
I'm running away from all this pain you put me through
I asked a scholar to show me the path
He whispered in my ear
His words of wisdom all fell flat
So now I've wound up here
The prophets are dead and the scholars are red from embarrassment
Your God's not the one who heals the sick and the dying
He's the one who will be trying to hide
Like a thief in the night

THAT STARTLING LOSS OF SELF

This record was perhaps my most self indulgent. I think we recorded in five different studios. The drums were done in Lubbock, then re-recorded here because the studio in Lubbock clipped every single microphone. I recorded with a friend of mine named, Matt, who is an insanely talented dude. He wrote all of the drums on the album and recorded the first round of pretty much everything with me in his basement. He and I had super similar musical influences and he naturally understood and improved upon what I wanted from this record. He also introduced me to Curb Your Enthusiasm, for which I am eternally grateful.
Thematically, this record was me trying to deal with loss. Loss of friendships more so than romantic relationships. In that way, it's kind of an island in the discography and one that is tough for me to look back on. That time in my life wasn't a very pleasant one. I struggled with being a good human back then and I'm very thankful that phase of my life is over. I hope that I've grown a great deal since discovering alcohol and having my first brush with popularity.

Mash Red (White Fences)

I've been looking for a song
Been pacing around this empty apartment wondering
Do the walls still sing the songs we used to write here?
Do the floors creak and sway beneath excited bouncing feet?
Will the light from the center of the living room shine across our screaming faces?
And will the empty rooms still beat as sweet as when our music overtook its tired frame?
I'm still alive but only just
Smile once, remember us
When we were younger bold and free
Eyes still wide but blind to see
This filthy world for what it is
Broken homes with white fences
God I'm looking for a song
That swelling chill that runs from one end of this city to the next one
I can hear it inside these coffee shops and bars
Feel its heat rise and fall every time I play guitar
When your name is the one I always burn
I remember how that burning used to calm

Home

When home becomes more than just the bricks you used to live between
And those dirty glossy magazines
And your paper painted families
With open arms they run to you
You know dear when you leave you will be free
Cause my heart became my mother's arms
Where she used to be
If I break, just don't tell my family
Cause they don't need to know
Just how far I've fallen
I need you in this moment
The net I wove it crashed
It fell around me
There's an empty spot on the floor
Where your brother used to lie
He'd protect you from the night
And all those creatures underneath your bed
And hiding in your closet
They keep you from your nighttime sleep
But you know my dear when you leave you will be free
But my heart became my father's arms
Where he used to be
As we break down and fall
All we need now is love
All I need now is a family or friends
We'd have each other
We'd lie to each other
We'd wait for each other
But I don't need anything at all

Into The Wild

Bring yourself back down dear
We've woven a net to catch you if you fall
Take the pills I left on your dresser
When you wake up I know you'll feel better but oh
You'll miss your home
When traitors tell your story
They make it sound so boring
So come on dear, let's make liars out of them
You can travel the world with your pocket grin
And a shattered heart through a camera lens but it's so far from here
And I wished on every star that I saw
In a car ride I took from Wichita
I swore I'd find your home
I've prepared a net and realize imperfections as you hurdle closer to my flaws
Swear to God I'm trying but I just can't catch them all
So high, so high even if I fall, I'm a light that shines I'm a shooting star you saw
And we turned this night to day

Love And War

I will breathe in air they said was toxic
Hope for violence when I walk alone at night
We carry heavy loads so we don't feel useless
We're just a couple punks up in North Vermont
All is fair
At least that's what they say of love and war
But you're somewhere
Between a bloody battlefield and
I can't fight
This air that's flowing into my lungs
So hold me tight
Hold me
You're a preacher's wife and father's thorn
You're the birthing tears of a child just born and
You can't hide behind those shutters that you've shut yourself behind
My mind still wanders more than ever
I must admit I love the fall
You wake up all alone and you're lonely
You wonder where we'll be when you fall
But I pointed out
All of your flaws ignoring mine
I took a knife
And gently cut along these dotted lines
To tear apart
Everything that we'd become
You were always the better son
You were always the better son

Waiting

My dear why are you praying?
Does the world seem that much brighter
When you're head down on your knees?
Does the open book on the altar
Miss the pages that you tore out to give me?
The children you left playing in the lobby
Didn't notice the tears on your cheek
And I've gotten so much better at playing the victim
And missing my family
I'm the nervous apprehension of a burden you won't mention
Under covers in our bed at night
I'm tracing rhymes and lines in the freckles 'cross your spine
We're both waiting for your God at midnight
But a call down the hall and a knock at the door
From the workers at the hospital
Emptied a room with a view
They're taking down pictures of you
That your mother said kept her smiling
When all she seemed to hear was bad news
Find her sipping on wine in the heavens
She always loved to have a good time
You live and love beauty the same way she did
That's how we fell in love the first time

Faith And Hope

I still hold hope for days when "hope"
Is more than just a word between close friends
Who lie and hide behind each other's backs
I still believe in us
Faith and hope are friends not lovers
Hide yourself behind the covers
Good things never come to those that wait
A crowd gathers to ask how
They could help mend a broken heart
Well the knife in my spine would be a pretty fine place to start
What are you waiting for?
Just give up now it's over
You're the darling in a tower hoping for a savior
Praying that your God will come
Yea you're hoping that your God will come
But He never comes

Subways

I want to walk through subway tunnels holding your hand
Empty change from our pockets for the homeless and the kids
Then we'd leave the subways for the streets of downtown
Your converse on the pavement is the night's only sound
We're just a couple kids with dreams too big for our heads
The plans we had for summer hidden underneath your bed
And on a map I drew out lines for all the places that we'll go
Hired a plane with buried treasure cause you're scared to take the boat
When I look in the mirror I wanna see
The broken child inside of me
But when I look in these eyes I don't recognize
Anything at all
From my child's eyes
The rain fell soft, you made a cup with your hands
You said the lights on 8th always made you wanna dance
I took leaf I found that was shaped like a heart
You said you loved the way the rain turned everything into art
A little brown book beside my bed
Filled with words from prophets and things my father said
Through the rain on the street that reminded me
Of the place downtown where we used to meet
Pretend for once that we are children
Yea we're still children

Exaggeratedly Lengthy Title, Desperately Trying To Sound Witty... (Part 7)

In your shortest skirt
With widest eyes
Mind sharp racing waiting on the perfect guy
To come along this lightless street
Then your mind starts racing as he sweeps you from your feet
Play it out like a scene from a movie
Make it romance only scripts give
Take your time dear we aren't in a hurry
Look into her eyes like you mean it kid
It's all about a camera lens
And in your dark eyeliner
You take the stage
Lines rehearsed now every verse
Spat out as bloody bait
To an unknowing crowd
With your clever lines
We're both all wondering
How you thrive in the limelight
Kill us off like a victim
Make it so discreet
Hold the knife like a lover with a brother lying underneath your feet
I wonder where you've been I'll take you where I am
I wonder where we'll be when you find out
When the lights come down I'll follow you out
I wonder
Who is this scene for?
The lighting is off and it's too much to ignore
I wonder where
I wonder how
I'll break you down
I'll find you out
Just tell me what I need to do next dear
It's all about the camera lens

Esprit De L'Escalier

You were the light at the end of a tunnel
That ended up being the sun
You were the fading light of my vitals
As soon as the doctors were gone
Break break me down with you
Tell me you need the truth
Tell me you lived with a lie
Tell me your lover is just your cover
Well babe I will be your lie
I will be your lie
Your smile breaks for any man that you see
When you walk down the road do you follow me?
And it's New Years all the time here
I still feel this winter air
It goes straight to the bone
I drink just to remember how you taste
Sangria on my lips reminds me of your hips pressed tight
So tight against mine
These city lights all burn the same
If only winter left as easy as it came
God knows I forced myself to try

Cain And Abel

Smoking gun and severed ties
The brother you preferred is dead and I
Have this blood of friend look for his keeper
From the time when we were children
Playing army with sticks bent like guns
In your parent's home I was forced to grow
But I was loved just like a son
Take a prayer to your grave
Swear I washed you away
But I can still smell your blood
Hear your tears as I end what we'd begun
I realize now I'm not Abel
Cause Cain was the selfish one
I buried you next to the raven
That God sent to hide his son
I'll find what it is that's inside of you and hurting
I'll tear open this earth just to beg your forgiving
Whisper sweet words that I always feared saying
Yea, all of this was my fault

Your Children Play With Matches

Your children play with matches in a house made of sticks
While their father was gone on a business trip
The danger wasn't blatant nor the children very wise
When asked who to blame
The father points his finger at his wife
Wear your sins
Swallow your revelries
Pray to your God
Promise you learned to believe
Your child waits in airports taking photographs of families
His backpack near a book read to him before he sleeps
If waterways and tunnels can be built with only sand
Grab a pail and a shovel and I'll make my amends
At least until it rains
Unsure and wild with our feelings
I'll be too impatient to hold the flame
So watch it burn
Watch it burn
Every light burns the same
Cause everyone I know is dying they just give it different names

Disaster

Her tears streaked mascara in the bathroom stall
Her hands shook, bracing on the green hued wall
She's scared because she thinks that love is gone
She's scared because she thought she'd found someone
She's scared because she held within her tiny painted hands
The plus or minus answer to everything she'd planned
And she falls
To the floor
Salt kissed raindrops crashing down
Her agony it paints the ground
And she screams
A silent plea
She wasn't ready
And this isn't right
Her breaths come faster
She's a frantic disaster
My friends Kevan and Trey
Were there the day you told me
We shared a drink and I
Watched the world crumble down
Outside my parent's window
We dug through the rubble just to watch you go
You'll be just fine
That's what you're good at
String me along
That's what you're good at

WITNESS MARKS

This was the record that brought me back to music. I had taken a long hiatus and because of that, kind of assumed I was done.

I was an IT guy now.

Not an artist.

I worked at Region 16 with my friends Matt and Jordan. We spent chunks of our days writing diss raps to each other in Google Hangouts. (It was a hard job)

These gradually escalated to the point that Matt and I decided we needed to go halves on an audio interface and build a cheap studio to record diss tracks for real.

This was one of the cheaper impulses we had.

Another was brewing our own beer.

Matt has fantastic ideas.

After a few joke tracks he suggested that I try and make another record. Like, That Startling Loss of Self. He has been remarkably supportive of my emo band and is the only human still spinning "Faith and Hope" from that record with enough regularity that I've made at least 15 cents from Spotify over the last several years.

I had some songs written with no intention of doing much with them. It was cathartic to play and write but I didn't really have a desire to trudge through the recording process again. Remember, Loss of Self was five studios and a chunk of money and emotional energy. It wasn't a fondly remembered process.

I recorded in my room with our rap setup. I suck at mixing so when I was done with the tracks I reached out the GOAT, Nicholas Schmitto. I had shot his senior pictures and spent time in the studio with him before. He shocked me by offering to help with the entire project for free and we put out a record together that kickstarted a friendship I'm eternally grateful for. I dig the songs on this album, but the biggest thing that I gained from this record was a rediscovery of my desire to create and my now best friend/producer/Call of Duty carry, Nick.

Spotify

I know we haven't kept in touch
I know you don't like me all that much
In fact, I'm sure you hate me
I still flip through pictures of you
Thinking back to nights we lived through
Flip your hair from left to right
Stay up painting late at night
And I hope that sometime
You'll hear my song on your spotify
Right after Sia's chandelier
On a playlist only you could hear
The hopeless empty in my voice
Please just let me be your noise
I'm not clever enough to beat those other boys you like
I'm a college drop out
Overworked and underwhelming
I'm only good at being charming
For the first couple of months
I'll lead you to my bed
I'm lost in my own head and
I'll leave you in the clutch
All of the nails in the walls from the pictures we hung there
I'm sure that there's a metaphor in there somewhere
But you burned bright the bridge between our hearts
Picked out the ashes and called it art
I miss your smile most at night
Alone in bars blurring my sight
Drowning out your memory
By trading my sobriety
Darling, lie to me
Subtle brush strokes light touches
Everything is undone
I still feel the bombs and fallout
Everything is undone
My home is just empty walls now
Everything is undone

Hazel's Song

There may be a light out there somewhere that I couldn't quite see
I found the world in the eyes of a child
They say she looks just like me
Poor thing
I hope you end up better than I have
I hope you avoid all the mistakes of your dad
I won't ever let you fall
I'll burn the world before you tumble
I'll keep you safe here in my arms
You won't ever have to be alone
Here in my arms girl you're home
I find myself wishing I was wiser and wealthy
I'll hand you the keys to this planet
And watch you sleep oh so soundly
Poor thing
While you continue to age
More lovely each passing day
More wonderfully kind in the words that you say
If everything fades away
If you wake unsure which road to take
If you lose yourself finding yourself along the way
With me you're home

Serendipity

You serendipitous wonder
Blind me to the world we live in
Take your hands, laid soft upon my face
Whisper visions in my ear
I fear I might forget the way you taste (like cigarettes and mistakes)
Just stay close and honest
Break free when you tire
Of the pieces left of me
You won't feel the slightest
Hint of something like a heartbeat
You'll just feel me
You resplendent marvel
Take away that weight I've felt for so long
Heavy heart and mind to match
Sleep more soundly than we should have than we
Would have thought
Than we
Could have thought
Listen to Yellow while the jukebox plays
Chris Martin's gonna sing on your wedding day
Taste of smoke under neon lights
Morning trying hard to chase this night
She might be right
We'll see
She might be right
And I'll be
Tasting like cigarettes and mistakes
Taking everything that she lets me take
She might be right
But I'll be
Wrong
Flawed and sober
She might be right
Even as I hold her
She might be right
But I won't feel a thing
I might be a monster
She didn't lie
She might be right
But I won't feel a thing

Acost

Acost you with plans of escape and travel
Listen to my drunken babble
I'll stumble right into your heart
I'll tear you apart
This young man found a God
This God just found him wanting
The wanting left him empty and alone
Hollow men just looking for a soul
I've got words and little else
I'm not the creature but the shell
Left after something new has been made
She said
Love is something that we make
It's a molded, fragile clay
Wouldn't you agree?
And this creator showed you me
Such blatant awful cruelty
I'm not fit for perfection such as yours
Fallen angels played by God like they're just toys
We get lost in the noise
Darling take my hand together we'll flee
We'll swim forever through the apathy
The whole world feels right when you're with me
I'll be that rock in stormy seas
Upon which you crash here near the reef
This ship will sink but we'll float on and on and on
Don't rely on me
You're the light and beauty in everything I see
Don't rely on me

Growing Up

I wanna grow old with you
Maybe through our twenties
But when we hit thirty
We just won't know what to do
You'll grow bored of love
And try out lust
Like all old women do
I'll get jealous and drink myself to sleep
We were kids
Having kids
Breaking our promises
Growing old is hard to do
Maybe if we leave this town
We could find a place to figure our shit out
But our kids will stay the same
Victims of our growing pains
I wanna take you someplace nice
To sign the papers from your lawyer and talk about our daughter
As though we've never met
You'll smile politely
And pass the check
Maybe someday my daughter will forgive me
For all of my mistakes and all the things that I've done wrong
I'm sorry darling, I was trying to be strong
I'm just as lost as ever and stumbling along
Forgive me darling
It was you I was thinking of all along

Gas for the Heater

I'll admit to whispered prayers in quiet rooms
Silent in my mind screaming at your tomb
I'm not a good enough man to pick up all your slack
Like saviors and creators I'll just turn my back
Asleep under stars in a cold old beater
We don't have money for the gas for the heater
The blankets on your arms don't provide much warmth
And I'm wishing I was wealthy or that faith was a hearth fire
I'm trying my hardest to wear your shoes
Doing all the things my betters tell me to
Cold stone statues standing at the gate
Don't bother telling me
Cause I know it's too late for me
Pray for me
Won't you pray for me?
I used to listen to a God that told me how to love,
Now I'm looking in myself and disappointing my family,
Holding on to the feeling just to keep some sanity
When I'm gone
The earth might swallow me whole
In a box built sturdy with hands whose craft is hard sold
When I'm gone
I'll float right up to the sky
Look your God in the eye
Words of redemption never crossed my lips
I won't be starting now
Stand your ground

My Friends

I was gonna grow old with good friends and better company
Find a girl and fall in love
Maybe beg that girl to marry me
I'd get a job, something with my hands
Something worthwhile, maybe make a little difference
My friends all moved away
Packed bags and simple goodbyes
The songs I write now sound more hollow
A mirror to the empty in my eyes
Since you left I've found and lost love
My daughter gets brighter with each and every day
And more beautiful all the same
She's the fear and purpose in everything I do
I want to make her proud and I'm trying my best to
Best efforts, lost contact
We were young and oh so foolish
If you were here
If you could see
You'd all be disappointed in me

I DON'T LIKE ME EITHER

I worked on this damned album for almost 2 years. And you are absolutely right, the quality can't possibly reflect the amount of time invested.
I feel like there are tons of weird cliches people use when talking about a record.
"This is my most honest album"
"It's a snapshot of the last year in my life"
"I'm bearing my soul in these lyrics"
Or whatever.
And as trite as it may feel, that's all true. I'm super freaking proud of this album. It was WORTH it to record four different revisions. It was worth it to rework drums in the final hour and it was absolutely one of my favorite experiences in music being able to spend time in a Dallas studio with my best friend, Nick, laying down guitar and vocals for an entire day. I drove down on Monday and stayed the night in the coolest bachelor pad you can imagine. I'm not exaggerating here, it's a beautiful home occupied by two music producers and two retired dudes. It was a dream and just so fun hanging out, playing Call of Duty, and talking trash with a bunch of friends. The next day we woke up early and headed to Fifty50 Studios about an hour away because Dallas people all enjoy getting onto the same roads at the exact same time to honk at each other and just hang out. It's cool from a community aspect I guess but honestly, not a fan.
The studio was immaculate and over the hours we worked there, I

desperately attempted to look as though I was better at guitar than I really am in front of Nick and the other engineer, named Aaron. Nick buzzed into my monitor at one point and said, "Hey, if you spend three years on your next record maybe you'll be able to learn all of your guitar parts." So yea, they knew.

After eight hours we had nailed the parts and the vocals and I felt amazing. You know, that first-mowed-lawn-of-the-season-as-a-new-dad kind of amazing. Kicked back in a chair with a cold beer and freshly green dyed New Balance 479s. I was done with my part for the album. This thing is actually gonna come out soon. No really. For real this time.

The drive back to Nick's Bachelor Heaven was an hour long and, as is generally the case with Schmitto, filled with incredibly rich conversation. We talked about God, and economics and girls. We discussed fear and death and so many things I just don't get to work through all that often. None of us, it seems, are able to discuss much of consequence without the aid of memes and a keyboard to hide behind. It was refreshing and more so even than the album, lifted my heart and my head. He's a very good friend and an even better human.

We ate Chick-Fil-A as it is both fast and delicious. Policies against the gays be damned, they make a wonderful sandwich. I may have insinuated that Dan Cathy could shoot me in the chest and I'd pick up some nuggets on the way to the hospital. I try to balance it out with angry political posts on twitter.

I drove back to rillo with a lemonade and chocolate chip cookie and the company of several serial killer podcasts that kept my heavy eyes open for the boring 6 hour drive.

This trip was important and served as a reset of sorts for me. If you're reading this, I assume you care about the record in some small way and I genuinely hope you dig it. It's more authentic than I have ever felt comfortable being and I believe a great deal of that comfort comes from working with a friend like Nick. I wrote this at a very strange time in my life and it was cathartic to explore the new fears I've been able to unearth as a teenager trapped in the body of someone rapidly approaching middle age. I hope you dig it, and that it resonates, but for me, the important piece is that I finished this damn thing. And I did.

Check it out on Spotify or whatever inferior streaming platform you may use. And if you are in need of a talented producer with an ear for hits, please hit up NUERA BEATS. Thanks for hanging around this long, and for listening to my songs. You all are amazing.

Lumineers

They keep playing Lumineers on the radio
And I
Still sleep with the fan down low
And I
Still dream about your hands all over me
I stumble 'round your side of town
Hit you up when the bars get loud
I'm just so lonely here without your company
I know that you may not be able to tell
But right now, I'm feeling a little unwell
That's Matchbox 20
Slam it
I still love you, but dammit
We never had a chance at all
Never had a chance you left before we could fall in love
I keep singing Cleopatra in my room
My bed still smells of your new perfume
I'm sick of chasing you with things I write
Knowing that I don't ever cross your mind
And it's your nonchalance that's been killing me
Oh we could just dance, dance dear, Thnks fr th Mmrs
That's Fallout Boy I think
Either way I guess we drink
We never had a chance at all, we never had a chance you left before we could fall in love
We were filling our lungs with summer
Tangled hands craving one another
Every empty bar still plays the same damn tune
Echoing the broken parts of you
and me
Eternally
Just you and me
Echoing
I know you don't think about me at all
But you're in everything I write so please just sing along
That's just love songs I guess
My heart is breaking through my chest
We never had a chance at all
Never had a chance you left before we could call it
No we never could call it "love"

Twitter Girl

Even though you're gone I still wish you the best
I'm still out here chasing red heads
Feeling depressed
Acting like I'm special
Like no one else has loved
Chasing dreams that I've had since fifteen
Never growing up
But in a jazz club, downtown
Hands in mine our heads in the clouds
The moonlight caught your eyes
That measure by which beauty's defined
My heart shook through my ribs
Those intangibles between two lover's lips
Yea, I'm still drinking myself to death
Treating barkeeps and their liquor
Like my therapist
Sharing all my secrets
With every anxious sip
Oh my songs were so much better back before I was so inebriated
I'm intoxicated with you
I could be air in your lungs
Let me be air in your lungs
Breathe me in
I'll be oxygen
I could be that hit
Just take me in
Wild at heart
Written on your arm
I should have known better
I should have known from the start
Wild at heart
Written on your arm
I held too tightly
And now you're gone
I could be air in your lungs
Just let me be
I could be

Winona Rider

God bless Winona rider for the things she took away
Normalized the idolized
Made all this feel okay
I just wanna say thanks
I just wanna be a celebrity
I want people to know my face
I want to be famous told you
Someday, I'll get my mic snatched by Kanye
But not today
Point that camera more direct
Get me in the frame
My whole life is a stream of consciousness
I need you all to see my brain
I'm not insane
Just desperate for your attention
Give me your attention please
Turn on the lights and clap
Sing along with me
I wrote this song for you
Lined the words up pretty
I sing out of tune but my producer makes me sound on key
I do it for the fans man
Of which I have maybe three
I wrote this song, sing along
I want everybody looking at me
God damn all the liars sharing bread with me
A smiling face so out of place
I see the blood between their teeth
Give me sympathy
I need your sympathy
I wanted to be a celebrity
So people would know my face
Thought I could be famous
If I rip off Brand New and Taking Back Sunday
But not today
Everybody look at me
I wrote this song for you
Lined the words up pretty
I sing out of tune
But Nick makes me sound on key
I do it for the fans man
Of which I have three
I wrote this song sing along
Everybody look at...

What Would a Martyr Do?

Yeah I wonder sometimes
About Jesus Christ
And if it bummed him that his dad just left him hanging on those sticks
Omnipotent savior chosen
Arms wide open
And his father wouldn't move
Your father wouldn't move
I'm just saying I'm a dad and that's not something I could ever do
I wonder sometimes
What it must be like
Up in heaven chilling killing time there with the chosen few
Hanging out
Complaining 'bout
The songs we sing and how
There really isn't all that much to do
Oh I'd miss my friends in hell
Cause heaven ain't the same here without you
If I make it to those pearly gates
And I don't see you
I'll give the finger to Saint Peter
Say I need her
Crank the heater
And jump into the flames to find you.
I saw those holes in your savior's hands
The one in my heart is shaped like you
So what should I do?
Hallelujah
I'm under your spell
And looking like hell
Floating the river styx to get to you
My halo and wings
Are such fragile things
I'd rather feel stronger next to you
Cause all of my dreams
Are imperfect things
Without the light and truth of you
So what the hell would Jesus do?

You Deserve Better

I'm really self-conscious about how few drugs I've tried in my life
While you were snorting coke off of that honor student's tits
I was busy playing Tony Hawk's Pro skater in my best friend's basement
While you were getting high on all the magnificence of nature
With five or 6 of your closest friends and some LSD
I was
Stumbling
I was stumbling
Through awkward conversation with the only girl that would talk to me
While doing dishes in the back of a Marble Slab Creamery
I worry dear
I'm just too boring to attract, someone as interesting
And clever
And honest
And worldly
And funny
And pretty as you
Cause I've only got this one tattoo
I'm really scared about how I might screw up my daughter
She got a really rough hand when she got me as her father
I was never all that great at taking care of me
The world is just an ocean and I'm drowning in the sea
But all at once I held her and the waters went calm
I may feel like I'm drowning but we will float on and on and on
She may deserve better but she got me
I'll die building this boat so she can float to safety
The water rises but darling don't you worry
You may deserve better but you got me
I'm just tryin to build a boat
To get us both to safety
So you turn out better, brighter than me
She deserves better
So much better than me
She'll turn out better
So much better than me
You'll see

Resonant Echoes

It's in the resonant echoes of the tired and young
Replacing fire and flame with the tangle of tongues
Two hollow shells tone deaf, and dumb
The hopeless rejection of the songs we once sung
We can't fight fire with clinical depression
Choke on these pills ignoring the lessons
We can't fight fire with empty rejection
Of those songs we once sung
Yea this future we've created has always freaked me out
Telling children the solution is a mushroom cloud
On the populous soil of a foreign land
Toss some teens in an airplane
Boots in the sand and call it God's plan
Nation blessed and swinging his rebuking hand
It's God's plan
So we'll sing hallelujah in a gang vocal chorus
You can't ignore us anymore
The Gods won't reach down
From the comforts of heaven
This armageddon still sounds
Just like the love we found
In those songs we once sung

Quit Praying

She said quit praying to your God
He don't care for anyone
Especially people like us
I said darling I agree
Cause here with folded hands
Your God won't answer me
So I quit praying to God
Never had much consequence
Didn't even give it much thought
He prolly needed a reprieve
From all the crying children
Begging for His love on both knees
In the places you keep Gods
Those secret parts inside your heart
In the prayers you send when the world feels most dark
I'll be
Drifting farther
From your God and Father
Leaving this place and never coming home
Cause when you're gone
The world feels so alone
The world is echoing so much louder now you're gone
And I'm alone

Kennady

I'm in love with this girl in Vegas
But I can't make her stick around
She left me for someone famous
I can't say that I blame her now
So I try my best to fill my time
But everything here reminds me of her
Across this God forsaken city
But girl when those lights and glam burn out
And you grow tired of the buzz
I hope someday I could convince you
To stay close and keep me honest
Tell me that you're fine
Swear to God you love me
Just one more time
We could have each other
The world you and me
You're my
My Kennady
Now she's dating some magician
Playing shows around her town
I've seen her she's still a vision
The only perfection that I've found
Cause even though his arms now hold her tight
She deserves much brighter
Than the glow of something pretty
You sing sing sing to Hamilton on the drive home
Can't keep my hands to myself
Or keep my eyes on the road
The beams of moonlight luminesce along your skin
I can't catch my breath
I don't know where we've been
They said my songs were better when I was alcoholic
Chasing girls with my lyrics
My liver going toxic
They said my songs were better when I was more ironic
Hating everyone I love
Drowning in gin and tonics
But look at me now
You were right
Just look at me
The lights and glam burned out

Chum the Waters

Chum the waters
Prepare for the slaughter
We are hungry
Lost at sea
A break in the base of the boat you float in
The water just flows and flows and flows in
It goes the way we all go
Beneath the currents and under the waves
I'm a ghost smelling blood and I haven't forgotten the taste
Cause you're here in my teeth
I'll be a predator
And you'll be so lonely
Lost at sea
These high waters
I'm scared for my daughter
Forgive her please the sins of her father
I try to protect but the world is losing its grip
I'm feeling unsteady I fear we all might
Slip
The one you thought would protect is baring his teeth
The one you thought you loved turned out to just be me
A disappointing shell just dragging you all to hell with me
Please forgive me

Apocolyptic Lovers

I've saved us a little bit of money
Always prepared for the worst
Socked aside some cash for us to use
You call me a pessimist
And tell me I'm the worst
Call me a fool
You tell me your ex was a lot more cool
But when those bombs start dropping
And the skies catch fire and rain
My arms however feeble
Will hold your shaky frame
Your shaky frame
You said that you're tired of hiding
This war must be over soon
Clawing at the walls that keep us safe
You tell me that I'm crazy
You say you're leaving soon
Whisper you're through
You tell me your ex would know just what to do
Now that the world caught fire
Flames are the catchlights in your eyes
We won't waste time on shelter
Cause you're the safest place I'd hope to find
Come close dear they won't take us alive
And I don't mind
When those bombs stop dropping
And the world is empty again
My arms will still be wrapped around you
You're all that matters in the end
You're all that matters dear
This is the end

Derek Porterfield

Coral

And you probably don't pray to Jesus
Saviors aren't really your style
You get nervous when walking by churches
And there's little a devil in your smile
You likely lie on your taxes
And talk shit about all of your exes
Cause they couldn't keep up
No they couldn't keep ya
No they couldn't keep you
But they're not like me
Take my hand dear I swear that we could leave
Somewhere far from this mediocrity
Somewhere close to the ocean
You'd love the sea
Somewhere perfect
Just like you for me
You're cut from the cloth of Exodus
Always running away
And I still give chase
I miss your taste
There's no God up in heaven that could part these wild seas
Those greatest expanses between you your faith and me
But I've built a raft dear and I'll brave the waters
There's room for us both take my hand come with me
Now I'm shipwrecked
Under the currents
All I regret
Is ever learning your savior's name
He won't care for me
Shipwrecked
I welcome the waves in
With every breath
The tide it keeps turnin
My hands are clasped
Holding you close to me
It's been years since I've prayed to Jesus
Played the savior for far too long
My cape is all worn out and torn up
And all I've got left is this song
I get bored when I'm reading the scriptures
Cause you were the light that I need
You fill up the spaces and your lovely face is
The only God in which I believe
Please run away with me

Smelted Circle

Smelted circle of rose and yellow
You left on my counter near the sink
Oh I've never fallen so far before
But I've flirted here
Feet near the brink
I never think
Your eyes are cold and clear
Those scratches in their corners are gone
Found you crying near your suitcase
You were pulling your jacket on
Empty boxes with colorful edges
House out front with the clean kempt hedges
We'll paint different pictures this July
All the colors you left in my home
Are gone from my eyes
I know it's clear you're angry darling
You talk about it constantly
I still feel you in this home and
I never sleep
Darling give up the ghost
It's not a competition who loved who the most
Let it go
Let it happen
Let it go
These ghosts are laughing at you now

Lies and Light

The lies and light are all the same to me
Just simple little bits of subtlety
If it blinds your eyes and hides the darkness within me
Then the lies and light are all the same to me
The man in the pulpit's lying when he speaks
Taking money from the poor and those in need
Just to buy himself a home
On hill among the trees
Like the place he claims his savior hung to bleed
For sinners like me
Promise that you love me more than I do
Promise that you'll share your air with me
Promise you hate me more than I do
I'm so tired of struggling
I'm so tired of getting lost in your features
But don't worry, darling
I don't like me either

PLEASE LEAVE A REVIEW

Thanks for reading. As a musician, my dopamine is tied directly to attention and I appreciate you feeding the beast. Reviews on Amazon and Goodreads help me to reach more people and deliver small amounts of happy chemicals into my brain. So thanks for helping me approximate fulfillment with the fleeting feeling of a stranger's approval. I probably love you.

THANKS

First off, thanks to anyone that has jammed or shared my records over the years. It is a strange and wonderful thing to hear lyrics that I've written in my darkest moments being screamed back at me from people I now consider friends during shows I never believed I'd still be playing so many years later. I'm a lucky guy by any measure, and those of you that continue to support me have helped me to realize that luck, in the times I've felt blind to it.

I also want to thank my best friend Nick. He has recorded, mixed and mastered every Derek Porterfield and All of His Friends album and he is the most genuine and talented person I know. He also absolutely kicks my ass in Call of Duty. I'm admitting that publicly now. I love you brother, and I'm very glad to be making art with you.

My daughter, Hazel, is every bright part of my life and carries a joy with her that is rare, even among children. Her laugh is my favorite, her imagination is remarkable and she has my whole heart, forever.

Matt McCabe and Jordan Herring are the reason I make music as a full fledged adult. Without their encouragement during a time that we were writing some pretty vitriolic raps to each other and recording them in Matt's office, I would never have recorded the songs I'd been working on.

They're both incredible men, and so attractive that I try not to stand too close to them in public. I love both of y'all in a creepy way.

Without Carly Stewart, this book would have never been released. She was the first to read any of my new work and she picked the title. I have trusted her with more than anyone in my life and she is rare in both spirit and talent. I love her dearly. If you dug this, you should pick up her poetry book, "Wayward Fruits" on Amazon. It is absolutely amazing and raw and wonderful in all of the ways that good art should be.

Amanda Richardson was the first to provide feedback on this finished book. To say that she is the best hype girl in the world is to understate the matter a great deal. She has been kind and supportive despite having never actually met me. She is an incredible artist and friend and you should check out her work (including a piece she painted after reading this book) on instagram. @jayebird_

Andrew Monroe encourages me in all of my projects and has served as a level head in a world where such things are rare. His brutal honesty and fierce friendship helped to shape me into who I am now. So blame him. Joseph, Matthew, Bethany, Morgan and Donna are my family and have been unwaveringly supportive in years that most people in my life were not. I love them all.

My Mimi and Pawpaw have helped with Hazel during a year of uncertainty and strangeness for people with kids in school. They're wonderful with her, and indulge her (often obtuse) games with grace that I hope to have at their age. I love them very much.

Stephanie and Talon Meeks are some of the biggest supporters of not just the music, but *me*. I love their family and I love them. They make me feel like the rockstar I always hoped I'd be when I was younger and only slightly more foolish.

There are so many people I don't have space to include. Please assume that if you weren't in this section, I hate you and everything you stand for.

Made in the USA
Middletown, DE
07 May 2022

65311341R00080